# Difficulties in Applying for Social Security Disability

## Respectful Suggestions for the SSDI Application Process

By: James M. Lowrance © 2012

## Dedication:

*To the many 'sincere' medical patients in our beloved Nation, who struggle to pay their doctor and hospital bills and to provide a living for their families due to their physical or mental disabilities. May your sincere request for disability benefits be given due consideration and may you find sincere ears to hear your case.*

# TABLE OF CONTENTS:

## INTRODUCTION:

Why would a layperson like me want to write a short-subject book regarding the U.S. Social Security Disability Program (SSDI)? Part of the reason comes from my having corresponded with many fellow medical patients since year-2003 (as a forum moderator and via email correspondence), some of whom were very ill but unable to pay their medical bills, in order to receive further care or to continue employment to provide for their families.

On many occasions, some of these patients expressed to me, their desire to apply for social security disability but they were reluctant to do so, after hearing about a friend or relative who was denied benefits, after going through two years or more of the application process, only to receive a series of denial letters from the benefits administration, throughout the process.
The people I'm referring to, who were wary of the system and reluctant to apply for benefits after hearing about denials experienced by other genuinely disabled applicants, were not mildly disabled but legitimately and seriously disabled.

Many were thyroid patients (one of the health disorders I experience), who suffered complications from their disease, such as severe neurological deficits (i.e. from near-fatal Hashimoto's Encephalitis or from delayed treatment of severe hypothyroidism or who had lost a significant portion of their eyesight from Thyroid Eye Disease/Graves' Opthalmopathy).

Being a thyroid disease sufferer myself, with co-morbid health disorders, including peripheral neuropathy, chronic fatigue, anxiety disorder (with co morbid intermittent clinical depression) and persistent asthma, my heart went out to these individuals because I understood their struggles. I too eventually accumulated extensive medical expenses and increasing difficulty maintaining my employment due to worsening health problems and I knew for a fact that my physical and mental struggles were legitimately disabling me.

I eventually applied for social security disability benefits myself, after struggling for eight years to continue a level of employment that would provide for the needs of my own family.

A final determination by a hearing judge was made, granting me a fully favorable decision for disability. The approval was first stated to my disability representative by the federally-appointed judge over my case at the final hearing; the legal representative actually being referred to me by the office of SSDI in my state.

The written confirmation for my case has also since arrived, which provided me the absolute confirmation. The final decision I personally received regarding my application for disability benefits, is actually not as relative to the goal of this book, as are the suggestions I wish to offer regarding the review process itself that is undertaken for social security disability applicants.

A question that might arise in the minds of those who read this book, would be as to why, if I'm able to write books and receive income from them, am I able to receive SSDI benefits? The reason that this is the case for me, is due to the fact that I was already involved with online publishing and book publishing for years, prior to my applying for SSDI benefits.

I reported this as income I was already making when I submitted my application and the income has actually grown to some degree, over the year and a half since applying. For many years, as I was building my publishing works (starting in year-2004), I was working full time, at the same time.

My more gainful work outside of the publishing is what I eventually became unable to perform due to my medical disabilities. My published works, most of which were actually written, prior to my applying for SSDI, have grown in readership and commission-income (many of my works that are now books/ebooks were online for years, as multiple articles under ad-revenue arrangements) . I was also informed by a representative with SSDI, that due to my income from the publishing, being commissions/royalties, it is not actual employment and will not offset my monthly disability benefits.

Rather than receiving a W-2 tax report form, at the end of the year, I receive 1099 forms for royalties I earn from the publishing, which classifies it as "miscellaneous income", rather than as "employment income".

In the mean time, I have considerably less income than I had prior to becoming unemployed due to my illnesses, plus my medical expenses continue as well and so I am extremely grateful to be receiving the disability benefits.

At one point recently, I came very close to withdrawing from my own SSDI application, when it was in the final stage of review, in-fact when it reached the stage of a pending review by a hearing-judge and it was less than a month from the scheduled hearing; I seriously considered discontinuing it (I am thankful that I did not follow through with cancellation, with the decision being "fully favorable" for me).

I will give explanation as to my reasons for considering this decision in a chapter that follows, which will also further answer the question as to why I made the decision to write this short-subject book on the subject of the U.S. Social Security Disability Program.

It is my sincere hope that the words I offer in this book, contain proper perspective and that nothing contained herein, is perceived as unnecessary ranting or complaining on my part against what I believe to be a program that has literally saved lives and the families of its recipients but that my thoughts will rather add some intelligent, logical perspective to this very difficult subject.

If by chance my offering of these chapters makes even the smallest positive difference in the disability program for legitimately disabled medical patient applicants, it will have been more than worth the effort to publish them.

## CHAPTER ONE:

## The Benefits of Being a Contributing American Citizen

As an American, I have never been anti-government during my lifetime and I never will be.

## The Benefits of being an American

I have benefited from the support of my country's government as much as any other American citizen has, including the fact that U.S. military servicemen have maintained our freedom and protection, since our Nation's birth. Certainly I have also observed things that occur within the branches of our government that are disappointing and sometimes disturbing to me but overall, I am proud of my country's government.

It is a historical fact that over time, as the modern age came into full-swing, the U.S. Government implemented a number of programs that have been extremely beneficial to the people they have been provided for.

This includes things such as benefits for our active and veteran military servicemen, low income housing, free or reduced-cost medical care and mental health clinics for various groups of people (i.e. the chronically ill, Native Americans, other minorities, teens and the elderly).

Thank God for all of these much-needed benefits provided by our government and funded by a system of taxing that is generally well-balanced. The system is not perfect however and it is strongly disagreed-with by certain tax reform advocates and groups who feel it could be better-balanced in regard to the taxing requirements for different income brackets of American tax payers. Some disagreement is also expressed in regard to the percent of taxes required for the purchase of different consumer products.

Whether one agrees or disagrees with the system of taxing, the fact remains that this is the method used to provide benefits to those who are legitimately less-fortunate in our Nation.

## The Value of Social Security Disability

We also have a system of social security that is generally also a well-balanced program, that helps to provide for our elderly citizens at their retirement ages and that helps those who are suffering from periods of low income, that in many cases is by no fault of their own but that results from unforeseen and unavoidable circumstances. I will mention that media commentators and even some representatives of our government have stated that some Americans in the baby-boomer age-category may not have social security benefits available for them when they reach retirement age.

They state that this will be due to a slowly failing U.S. economy, unless preventative measures are implemented and followed, to reduce the current national dept. If this proves to be true, this would mean that some citizens in this category, receiving social security disability may find that these benefits will be the only ones they will see in their lifetimes. Certainly, we all hope that this does not prove to be true and that benefits will continue to be available for retirement-age people, for all future generations.

*Difficulties in Applying for Social Security Disability*

The current system also includes benefits for those who cannot continue to earn an income through employment, due to chronic or terminal illnesses they may develop, that disables them physically or mentally.

This is certainly a wonderful thing and it has saved many of its recipients from losing their homes and reasonable quality of life for their families and even from losing their lives early, by providing opportunity for continued medical care that would otherwise be impossible for them to obtain.

## The Deserving and the Scammers

With this said, there are also those policies practiced or enforced by the social security disability program for example that cause deserving applicants to be denied and in some cases, less-deserving or undeserving applicants to be accepted by the same benefits program. I wish to point out some of these policies, within the chapters that follow but I endeavor to do so, without appearing to be casting dispersions on the system as a whole.

I sincerely believe it is extremely important for legitimately disabled Americans to be cared-for in a country that takes pride in helping those who are less-fortunate -- not those who are looking for a free ride or for a chance to scam the system but who are truly and sincerely in need.

Even passages found in the Holy Bible, warn against catering benefits to those who simply do not want to contribute reasonably to society and to their own families. At the same time, the fact that these types of individuals certainly do exist, should never hinder the benefits that should be received by those who do truly qualify for them.

While I will mention serious difficulties for applicants that I see within our government's disability benefits program, I hope to do so, balanced with the fact that its continuance is essential for the survival of our chronically and terminally ill citizens, now and in the future.

# CHAPTER TWO:

## The Proper Screening of Disability Applicants

I would like to mention at the start of this chapter, that I realize the process of reviewing disability applicants by government workers and representatives, is obviously <u>very difficult</u> for those who are employed to do so; this is true of the pre-screening personnel, doctors who may be involved and for final-hearing judges as well. The difficulties involved are likely far more involved than most of us citizens realize and those who work for the system, must abide strictly by the laws and guidelines involved, regardless of their own feelings about them.

## Avoiding both Unfair Denials and Illegitimate Cases

Regardless of the difficulties involved, it is a government-developed program and everything possible should be done to avoid the unfair denials of legitimately disabled applicants and also to continue avoiding the approval of illegitimate cases.

Certainly, this is obviously what they endeavor to do and what they wish to be done in each reviewed-case when possible.

With this said, I would like to suggest a policy that might make this goal more achievable. While I am simply a layperson and not a government worker or official, I am a U.S. citizen and a taxpayer and I am simply exercising my right and privilege to make such a suggestion, which I hope at some point in the near future, will be given legitimate consideration by the Social Security Administration.

I cannot express how badly I feel for those individuals who are granted social security disability benefits, after being diagnosed with terminal illnesses that are expected to be fatal. Certainly these people deserve these benefits, first and foremost, to help them continue supporting their families, during their final years, months, weeks or even days of life. There are however, also those individuals with illnesses that are not expected to be imminently fatal but that cause them a great deal of pain and suffering or serious restrictions in their ability to function physically, at normal or relatively normal levels.

These folks can also deserve disability benefits, which were designed and implemented for these types of cases as well.

## Allowing logical/Intelligent Observations as well as Medical Records

Unfortunately, due to past abuses of the U.S. social security disability program from both sides (i.e. the granting of benefits to individuals with unproven or mild disabilities and applicants who apply but who are not actually disabled), some legitimately qualified individuals are now being denied benefits, due to their inability to sufficiently prove their level of disability via the allowed medical records.

If for example, an applicant's doctor has yet to provide a definitive diagnosis for a terminal illness and he or she is reluctant to do so, for fear that it will be proven to be incorrect at some point or the patient could not afford to follow-through with definitive diagnostic testing, the social security administration will in most cases view such a case as being unqualified.

This can be true in spite of the medical patient having obvious outward physical signs of disability and medical records that clearly indicate that a serious illness is being experienced (i.e. symptoms of organ failure, chronic blood loss or rapid muscle wasting).

The social security personnel, who are appointed to review such cases, must abide by strict guidelines and they are not given permission to make judgments regarding a case, that fall outside of them, such as using educated personal evaluations, apart from medical records. In most cases, they simply cannot look at something that is evident from a physical observation standpoint, if a patient's medical records do not confirm the obvious.

If for example, a person has strong indications of having a motor neuron disease, many of which prove to be fatal, within a few years of contracting them but the patient's MD or neurologist has not provided a definitive diagnosis, the most likely decision by case-reviewers, is to dismiss the possibility of a terminal illnesses.

Even if an MD's notes state that the patient has severe muscle wasting in one limb and that they have begun to experience difficulty with swallowing, talking or breathing, occurring co-morbid to the muscle loss, the least catastrophic reason for the applicant's symptoms would be the likely ruling by reviewers, with disability benefits being denied as a result.

Their ruling in such a case, might state to the effect that the patient has a simple mono-neuropathy that does not completely disable them or that they are simply experiencing the effects of bad physical conditioning, due to lack of exercise. They might also be viewed as experiencing a degree of psychosomatic symptoms, if medical records do not confirm a medical cause of their symptoms.

I will add that I believe this to be a scenario that can occur during the initial phases of the reviewing process and far-less likely to be something that would occur, should such a case reach the stage of going before a disability hearing judge, who would see the applicant in-person.

## Providing Disability Applicants Help with Medical Diagnosis

The patient in the scenario I have just described may be anguishing over the fact that they are financially unable to obtain the proper testing to receive a definitive diagnosis but the fact remains that they cannot make something happen, that is not possible for them to afford.

In my opinion, when reviewers can clearly see that a strong possibility exists for there being a terminal illness present in an applicant who has not received the proper diagnostic evaluation, as a result of inadequate funds, diagnostic medical services should be considered as a government-funded provision, so that potential life-threatening or severe chronic illnesses can be ruled out or confirmed. This type option could be provided to applicants suspected of having undiagnosed illnesses and made a requirement for those who claim to have serious undiagnosed illnesses but who may be attempting to scam the system or who may be experiencing a psychosomatic illness.

The result of such a policy, as generally described above, could be the better granting of benefits to those who truly deserve them but who have inadequate medical records and the better screening-out of those claiming to be chronically or terminally ill but who are mistaken or who are attempting to obtain benefits illegitimately. Referral for testing does exist within the SSDI program to some extent but this will usually be in regard to mental and emotional evaluations.

In some cases, medical evaluations/exams may actually be ordered, even in advance of a final hearing, where medical doctors are sometimes asked to attend to evaluate applicants but this doesn't happen for some applicants in need of them. I know this from the experiences related to me by extended family members and friends I have known, who were not offered medical evaluations and who were denied benefits.

Some were actually granted benefits later, when they reapplied and their medical conditions became more obviously disabling.

It is almost certain that this type of policy for more in-depth medical testing in cases where it appears to be obviously needed (but no afforded by applicants), for implementing into the disability review process has been suggested at some point and possibly at several points in the past. It is possible that some government officials involved in making changes to the system, have yet to approve them, due to more emphasis on screening-out applicants, than on making sure legitimate cases are not denied. I certainly cannot state this to be the case but the fact remains that such a policy does not exist to the extent I have described, after decades of the social security disability program's existence.

CHAPTER THREE:

## Why I Applied for Social Security Disability

In the year 2003, at age 40, I was diagnosed with autoimmune thyroid disease, which caused me to become hypothyroid (underactive thyroid gland). Before my diagnosis, I made several doctor-visits, complaining to them about multiple symptoms that I believed pointed to a medical condition (i.e. severe fatigue, joint and muscle pain, extremely dry skin, hives and mild swelling in my face).

## My Medical Diagnoses

### *Autoimmune Hypothyroidism*

Blood lab testing revealed two abnormally low thyroid hormone results, an elevated TSH level (a pituitary hormone that elevates with hypothyroidism) and I was found positive for two thyroid antibodies(cells from the immune system that attack the thyroid gland), with the level of one being nearly 500 points above normal.

I was started on treatment for the underactive thyroid, via hormone replacement therapy.

As the years went by however I found that I was experiencing widespread body pain and neurological type symptoms and I began the quest once again, to find out what was causing my unrelieved symptoms, in spite of being well-treated for my hypothyroidism (doctors worked with me to get the hypothyroid therapy optimized). I felt certain that another medical condition or possibly more than one was occurring co-morbid to my thyroid disease (together with it).

### *Peripheral Polyneuropathy, Myopathy and Non-alcoholic Fatty Liver*

I began to experience worsening pain symptoms in my arms and legs and my muscle-weakness, which manifested even prior to my being treated for hypothyroidism, was worsening. This problem was eventually revealed as a type of peripheral neuropathy (a neurologist also suggested "thyroid myopathy" as a possible cause of my muscle-weakness) however, in my case the symptoms developed a bit atypically -- not the type of progression usually seen with nerve disease.

After approximately two more years of increasing neuropathy and myopathy symptoms, I requested medical tests that might reveal the cause of my peripheral nerve symptoms. This included a brain MRI (negative for neurological diseases), an ultrasound of my liver (this one revealed that I had non-alcoholic fatty liver but no cirrhosis), a thyroid ultrasound (this one further confirmed my diagnosis of Hashimoto's autoimmune thyroiditis but no thyroid cancer found), blood tests for other autoimmune diseases and my vitamin levels (negative for co-morbid autoimmunity but positive for three vitamin deficiencies).

### *My Vitamin Deficiencies*

Vitamin tests revealed that I had vitamin D deficiency and an insufficient level of B12, which my doctor began treatment for via replacement vitamins. These treatments still did not affect improvement for my neuropathy symptoms, after many months and so I asked my doctor's office for a referral to a neurologist. All of the testing and doctor's visits up to this point, I paid for, out-of-pocket as a non-insured patient.

Just weeks prior to my getting set up as a new patient with the neurologist, my wife found insurance for me, through an underwriter for Blue Cross and they accepted me, even with my prior medical diagnoses. The coverage was moderate but my costs would be significantly lower than in years past, which accumulated into 1,000s of dollars each year. At the time of obtaining the coverage, we had paid all past medical bills in-full.

The neurologist diagnosed yet another vitamin deficiency I was experiencing via blood testing, this time being a very low level of vitamin E (near undetectable). This finding alone, could explain my development of peripheral neuropathy. I also had abnormal readings on a nerve conduction study that measures the amplitude of signals being conducted by large fiber nerves, further confirming nerve disease. The results showed below-normal and low-normal amplitudes on several of my large fiber nerves.

My vitamin deficiencies were further evaluated for a cause of them but it was determined that I did not have a malabsorption syndrome of any type.

I also do not have cirrhosis of my liver biliary tract, as a cause (biliary cirrhosis). In many cases, nutritional deficiencies can be caused by improper diet or can be idiopathic (no cause determined), the latter apparently being the case with my deficiencies (some medical research studies have shown that deficiencies are more common in people with thyroid autoimmunity).

## My Decision to Apply for Disability

After approximately six months of visits with the neurologist but with no treatment available for my progressed pain in nerves and joints and muscle weakness (myopathy), other than medication to help control the pain-aspect, my wife and I decided that I should apply for Social Security disability. In addition to my physical symptoms, my anxiety disorder, which includes aspects of both panic attacks and social phobia, that I had successfully coped with for many years, returned and had reached a severe level (in my case, fatigue and other physical symptoms can seriously affect my anxiety disorder). I resigned from a job I held for 16 years because even the driving involved in the work had become difficult for me.

This was due to weakness in my legs and feet, that occurs with any repetitive use of them (more severely affects my arms).

A deciding factor in my applying for benefits, included the fact that my nerve disease and myopathy had continued to progress and had especially worsened over a two year period. My tolerance for stress of any kind was very low and my symptoms, especially the chronic fatigue would flare severely with even mild stressors. I also developed persistent asthma with some flares being severe (i.e. asthmatic-bronchitis flares).

I had never drawn social security benefits of any kind; including no unemployment benefits at any point and my over 30 years of steady employment provided me with the qualifying work credits to apply for disability benefits.

**The Expected Initial Denials**

We knew to expect two initial denials of benefits once applying because we were even told this by representatives working for the office of SSDI.

This is due to the fact that they need a period of time for a process of thorough investigation of medical records. This is certainly understandable however, we didn't expect a period of time that would be two years in length (by the time benefits are received) and a very high probability of denial even in cases of significant reduction in one's ability to earn income to support self and family.

I will discuss my reasons for considering placing a stop on my own application, before a final decision was rendered, in the next chapter I will also include additional suggestions for the social security disability application process that again, have likely been suggested in the past but to this point, have not been implemented, possibly for a number of various reasons.

## CHAPTER FOUR

## Why I Considered Canceling My Application for Social Security Disability before a Final Hearing

I would like to make some important statements at the start of this chapter, so that my comments added afterward, in regard to nearly canceling my disability claim are not taken from a wrong perspective by the readers of them.

### Relying on the Government for Everything

The fact is that some citizens of our nation are actually too pro-citizen and they feel that we should all be catered-to by our government. They may be of the opinion that practically every need they have should be provided-for by the government, through compensation programs.

I am certainly not one from this camp of thought but I rather have always taken pride in being one who has contributed to the American society, to the best of my ability.

Because of my stance in wanting to be a contributor, rather than a recipient of benefits, unless they are absolutely necessary, it was a very difficult decision for me to apply for social security disability benefits. I felt to some degree, that this amounted to a plea for charity on my part and it struck me negatively in my pride and actually made me feel less-capable as a man for having to resort to it.

My wife would remind me when I pointed this out to her, that this simply was not the case but I found difficulty shaking this feeling and it also had a great deal to do with the reason I came very close to canceling my disability application during its final stage. I will add that no one employed by the Social Security Disability Administration, caused me to have negative feelings about applying for benefits, at any point during the process.

**Stigmas Attached to People who Apply for Disability**

It is also a fact that societal stigmas similar to what I have just described, are often attached to people who are approved for disability benefits.

I have personally heard people make statements in reference to someone receiving benefits, to the effective of "they don't look sick to me" and "they're just being freeloaders".

If a recipient is seen doing any type of activity at all, these types of statements can be heard being directed at them. Certainly this type of judging others comes from ignorance because those who make such statements cannot possibly know what another individual is going through, unless they review their medical records and interview them extensively, just as reviewers do, who work for the social security administration.

I personally have the outward appearance of one who is in good health and I could not help but to believe that this would be a factor when my hearing before a disability judge was scheduled. I have a neighbor for example, who I saw mowing his lawn just days ago, who was granted disability benefits some months ago. I know for a fact that despite his occasional activity, that he was treated for severe colon cancer, less than a year ago.

As mentioned in a previous chapter, there are certainly the freeloader types of individuals who attempt to scam the social security administration and some are actually successful in doing so.

Someone for example can claim they have a severe lower back problem that prevents them from standing or sitting for longer than a few minutes at a time.

A back injury in many cases cannot be confirmed as being present through medical lab testing, even when imaging tests are ordered for the patient. Muscle pain and rheumatic inflammation simply do not show up on medical imaging scans. Unless the condition results from an underlying disease, other diagnostic methods such as blood testing, will not reveal anything either.

These types of cases, when scam is involved, have made disability application policies far stricter as a result and understandably so. It has also made the process far more difficult for legitimately disabled people, with medical conditions that are difficult to diagnose.

## Medical Records and Doctor Statements

In my case, my medical tests confirm my
diagnosis of autoimmune thyroid disease (blood
tests and thyroid ultrasound), abnormal nerve
conductions (nerve conduction studies by a
neurologist), fatty liver(liver ultrasound) and
systemic inflammation (positive result on an ESR
blood test). Even with this, the extent of my pain,
weakness and disability is impossible to prove by
simply stating it to a reviewer, hence it was
required that a doctor supply a signed document,
listing the extent of my disabilities. I can again
understand the reasoning behind this requirement.
What I do see as a problem however, are those
applicants who have not been working for many
months and who cannot afford additional medical
check-ups or diagnostic tests to be ordered by
their doctors.

In these cases, when reviewers can see that
significant medical evidence has been provided,
that strong consideration should be given by the
social security disability administration, to
provide further medical evaluation to the
applicant, in order to render a more-informed
decision on these type cases.

While disability hearing judges do sometimes ask doctors to be present during a hearing, to help confirm or to challenge an applicant's medical claims, this is not quite the same thing as an exam conducted within a diagnostic setting (as mentioned previously, medical evaluations are provided in some cases but not in all cases that may merit them).

In my case, I provided two documents, one being filled-out and signed by my regular doctor and the other by my neurologist, stating that my neuropathy and myopathy hinder my ability to walk even short distances or to drive a car for more than short distances without difficulty, in addition to other mentions, such as my inability to lift objects of weight, etc... I was still asked to have yet another document filled out by my doctor, going into additional details regarding my daily activities, to provide at my final hearing.

The question arose in my mind at that point, as to how my doctor could possibly know how to answer some of these questions, unless I moved into her home for a period of a few days, so that she could observe me in more detail.

I do not add this statement for sarcasm (sincerely not), I simply add it, to point out that great importance is placed on medical test results, as should be the case and yet at other times, they seem to be given less significance by the reviewers of disability applications. I was eventually able to get the additional form completed by my doctor that repeated the extent of my disabilities.

## The Disability Application Time Element

Another major issue I see regarding the disability review process is the time element involved. From the time I first applied, until my final hearing was approximately 15 months. There is a five-month waiting period involved in the process, meaning that from the time an applicant submits an initial request for benefits, SSDI does not recognize those months as part of the applicant's period of disability.

The paperwork I received, giving details regarding my upcoming disability hearing stated that after review by the judge, his decision would be rendered to me in writing, by mail in 4 to 8 months.

Mine only took approximately 2 months, for which I was very grateful. With my previous steps of the process occurring at the maximum time limit given for them, adding up to over a year, the official final decision (in writing) arrived at approximately 14 months following my original application submission.

I know other SSDI applicants who waited 24 months for their approval to arrive and I know one applicant I became acquainted with via an online health forum, who has remained in the process for 5 years and continuing (they resubmitted new applications after final decisions on previous ones were not favorable for them).

I nearly opted to cancel the process, which by some opinion might have appeared to be a bad decision, with my having waited so long and with back-payment of benefits also pending, which will amount to a significant sum. The time element however, was not my only reason for wanting to stop the application process but it was a combination of several reasons as previously described.

I will also mention that the worsening/flaring of my anxiety disorder was making the hearing seem like an insurmountable task for me. I actually began to experience a severe dread and panic attacks, several days in advance of the hearing. These are aspects that are difficult for me to share in writing because in spite of my own search/research on the anxiety disorder subject (including my past coping success) and knowing that sufferers cannot help experiencing them, it is a point of embarrassment for me to admit my recent, severe struggles with it.

This is especially true with my having written a great deal on the subject in the past, to benefit other anxiety disorder sufferers (i.e. the saying comes to mind: "physician heal thyself"). I did in fact experience a severe panic attack during my hearing before the judge -- I simply became overwhelmed during the proceeding but my representative assured me that this helped the judge to understand more-fully, what I was going through (still it was extremely difficult for me to have other people seeing me experience this).

It should be understood that SSDI hearing judges are highly-qualified and they can spot the insincerity or dis-ingenuousness of an applicant, very quickly.

One of the reasons offered by the social security disability administration for the lengthy time element involved in applicant-reviews is due to their being so backed-up with cases to review. Even with this being the case, it would seem that solutions could be implemented to reduce this time period for applicants who continue to suffer a worsening of their financial status as a result of the extended period of waiting for a decision regarding benefits.

Even reducing the waiting time, to a total of six months for applicants who receive two initial denials, including any waiting period, would be far more tolerable (after a second contesting of a denial by an applicant, a hearing is granted before a disability judge). Applicants know that going to work during the waiting period will almost certainly result in a final denial.

Some will eventually do so however, in spite of extreme difficulty in carrying out work duties, possibly even at the risk of collapse or a worsening of their health condition.

Some may find that they have no choice but to secure employment, rather than to be unable to feed their family or to receive mandatory medical care if the decision on their disability claim is significantly delayed. I will mention that some applicants are considered for immediate benefits when they apply for disability (Supplemental Security Income -- "SSI") but they are required to meet financial requirements and these emergency relief type benefits are understandably temporary in many cases.

**An Unavoidable Change in Work Duties**

In my case, I did not consider canceling my disability application, in order to secure employment and at the time of writing this book, I remain unemployed although I do make income through other sources, including from my publishing projects as previously mentioned, which I have done since year-2004.

I also receive nominal income from royalty payments I make from an invention I patented and licensed in 1996 (See "About the Author", at the end of this book), which is very nominal.

When I received my first denial for disability benefits from the social security administration, they mentioned in the denial letter, that I could still perform certain types of work but specific suggestions were not given as to what type of work that might be. I feel that it would not take a great deal more time for the reviewers who send initial denials, to actually list job suggestions, in a general manner, to denied-applicants that they know for a fact do have significant disabilities.

I cannot imagine that they would feel that this might result in some type of liability placed on them, especially if the suggestions were for several types of work an applicant could look into. By adding this type of information, applicants may feel that the suggestion that they are still capable of work that will provide a living for their families, has legitimate basis, rather than coming across as kind of a slough-off.

It could also help to avoid their perception that there is an indirect implication that they are exaggerating their illnesses (I certainly do not believe this to be the intention of SSDI).

Let me add that following a final denial, applicants are offered vocational counseling by the SSDI administration that can help place them into jobs they can still perform in consideration of their limitations but information of this type this is not always offered by the reviewers who may give initial denials for disability benefits, that occur prior to a final hearing.

Also included in the first denial I received were comments that I felt were unsubstantiated. I say that respectfully but with sincere conviction. The reviewer stated in my particular case, that since my treatments began, which included my vitamin supplementation for deficiencies, that I was "doing better". This report of my doing better was not offered by me nor by either of my two doctors and in-fact my symptoms, including peripheral neuropathy had not improved but had actually worsened from the time of my initial disability application. Similar statements to this effect were also included in the initial denial letter.

I feel reviewers should be cautious not to add statements within a benefits-denial review that have not been reported to them by the applicant or by his/her medical care providers (this likely can be affected by the "interpretation" of how medical reports are worded by doctors and not the fault of SSDI reviewers).

## Should Partial Disability Benefits be Available?

If an applicant is obviously disabled to a significant degree but not as completely as to receive full disability benefits, it would be of tremendous value to applicant's who can still work but who will experience a significant drop in ability to earn an income, to receive partial disability benefits. Of course there are other options to help those who are unable to make gainful income to the fullest extent, such as the food stamp program (Supplemental Nutrition Assistance Program - "SNAP") and in some cases, medical benefits as well but these are actually welfare programs, offered through another department of the Social Security Department.

Also, when an SSDI applicant receives a favorable decision to receive benefits, they automatically become eligible for "SSI" payments as well (Supplemental Security Income) as I mentioned previously. This is from the Department of Human Services branch (DHS), which provides benefits payments to those who will also be receiving SSDI, based on their household income status. In some cases these added payments are temporary, until the applicant's SSDI payments begin arriving to them or they may even continue afterward at an adjusted-amount but this all depends on the applicant's household income (spouse income included).

If when an applicant first applies for SSDI, it is determined that SSI payments should begin immediately, due to their being at a low enough income to merit immediate benefits, these may actually start early into the SSDI review process. SSI benefits would also stop, at some point, should an applicant be denied approval for SSDI. Some elderly citizens who receive retirement-age Social Security, are also approved for SSI payments.

Here again, we see the great value in these programs for those who are in need of them.

Currently, partial disability is not available through the U.S. Social Security Administration and yet it is available through conventional insurance programs. I for example was granted disability through an insurance company, who is making monthly payments, directly to the lender who holds a lien on my vehicle (loan payments), that are slightly less than one-third of what my benefits will be through social security disability.

The insurance benefits were granted to me based on my medical records and I received the approval before receiving my first denial from social security (more than a year ago at the time of this writing), even with the fact that I applied for them both at the same time. I realize that much of this has to do with the social security system having much stricter policies and with the fact that benefits paid out by them are full-benefits, when approval is granted.

My benefits from the insurance company are smaller than the benefits of my social security disability claim.

However, this was due to the type of coverage I obtained from them and it is not partial disability benefits per se. The insurance representatives who reviewed my case, apparently judged my medical diagnoses as being sufficient to render an approval decision. The social security disability representatives however, felt that I had yet to offer enough proof of medical disability, which added many more months to the investigation/evaluation process.

The reviewers for social security disability cases are trained to find every possible legitimate reason to deny benefits to applicants and understandably so. While this policy is certainly not wrong within itself, an overly-biased stance toward eliminating government payouts of benefits, in some cases could result in some qualified individuals not being approved.

At the same time, if a reviewer is overly-biased toward applicants, this actually would result in illegitimate payouts of government funds and so it is somewhat of a dilemma from both sides.

The only solution to help prevent this type of problem is for both reviewers and applicants to be as thorough as possible with any information that is exchanged and to move forward with honesty and integrity.

## In Conclusion:

As stated in my introduction, the Social Security Disability Program is a wonderful thing provided by our U.S. government; it could however stand to be tweaked in certain areas that would help to keep legitimate applicants from being denied or from them giving up on the process before a decision is rendered for their cases. I am personally grateful beyond words for the financial relief the program has provided for me and my family and I am thankful that I did not give up on the process that rendered a favorable decision in granting me benefits.

Nothing is so perfect that it is beyond a degree of reformation and improvement but the officials and decision-makers have to be those who are willing to see changes of improvement made.

I personally feel that there are those who may feel that the SSDI system is nothing more than a strain on government funding. Those who see the necessity in the program however, are often those who have either experienced a medical disability of their own or they have seen it occur in a close friend or relative. This is where my own passion comes from in seeing truly disabled people helped by this essentially-provided program.

The value I see in SSDI, as funded by U.S. taxpayers, comes from experiencing my own disability and from that I have seen experienced by family and friends and by acquaintances I have corresponded with over the years, as a Thyroid Patient Advocate (a fellow patient attempting to help educate others with similar diseases to mine).

Our Nation has certainly experienced its own struggles as a whole, including recent economic recessions but I pray that these struggles will never cause a diminishing of our needed social security programs or a discontinuation of them but rather that they will be open to continued improvements for the future of our chronically and terminally ill U.S. citizens.
-*Jim Lowrance*

## About the Author:

I am a husband, father, grandfather and lifetime contract salesman, with experience in health writing that began in 2004. I completed theological studies with Liberty University in 1996. I formerly served as editor and forum moderator of Thyroid Health for a major multi-topic content site and as a general health writer for another, where I received Editor's Choice Awards for my articles on health subjects.

In 2003 I was diagnosed with hypothyroidism; "Hashimoto's thyroiditis" being the cause. This autoimmune form of thyroid disease that causes destruction of the thyroid gland resulted in my also developing "Chronic Fatigue Syndrome", due to a compromised immune system with severe co-morbid "Adrenal Fatigue". I also suffered severe anxiety symptoms, including panic attacks early into the onset of Hashimoto's thyroiditis (Hashitoxicosis). A common heart murmur I was diagnosed with in my teens called "Mitral Valve Prolapse", also worsened in severity of symptoms, with the development of these other health disorders.

My eventual receiving of diagnoses was a difficult process with proper diagnostic testing not being ordered by the first doctors I sought treatment from. These types of issues were inspiration for me to become proactive in my own health care and to self-educate myself on these health disorders, which I have done extensively since 2003. I now enjoy sharing this information with other patients experiencing my same health disorders.

During the early 1990s, I marketed an outdoors product I invented and that I formed a small corporation to patent, manufacture and sell called the "Rod Floater" (now a registered Trademark). I traveled the U.S. making presentations to groups of Wal-Mart zone and district managers and received authorization to sell the product in two regions of Wal-Mart stores for five years.

I also sold the product to Bass Pro Shops, Cabela's and Academy Stores, all of which still carry the product and I landed a national promotion for the product with Kerr-McGee Oil Company who began using the product to promote their outboard motor oil in 1992.

In 1996 I licensed the product to TTI-Blakemore, a major fishing tackle conglomerate, from which I am still paid royalties from sales of the product.

I invented and marketed five additional outdoors products, also getting these into Wal-Mart stores and afterward sold them outright rather than licensing them.

I learned a great deal about invention marketing during those years and was privileged to meet the CEOs of many well-known companies. I was also invited for television and radio appearances and met with the T.V. hosts of many fishing shows and was featured in the May 2001 issue of Inventors digest magazine.

www.ingramcontent.com/pod-product-compliance
Lightning Source LLC
Chambersburg PA
CBHW031332290526
45784CB00014B/2590